The
INTERNATIONAL
Book of
BEER

The
INTERNATIONAL
Book of
BEER

A GUIDE TO THE WORLD'S MOST POPULAR DRINK

BARRIE PEPPER

TODTRI

To Carolynne
who drove me to the pub
(and back again)

This book was designed and produced by
Todtri Productions Limited
P.O. Box 572
New York, NY 10116-0572
Fax : (212)695-6984

Printed and bound in Korea

ISBN 1-880908-46-8

Author: Barrie Pepper

Publisher: Robert M. Tod
Designer and Art Director: Ron Pickless
Editor: Nicolas Wright
Typeset and DTP: Blanc Verso/UK

CONTENTS

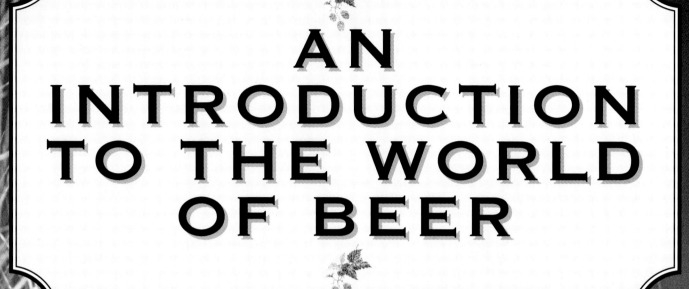

AN INTRODUCTION TO THE WORLD OF BEER

A monk hard at work brewing beer
c. thirteenth century

No drink in the world commands quite the universal respect of beer. Wines, spirits, ciders and other alcoholic beverages all have their adherents and advocates; tea, coffee and soft drinks are praised by their supporters, but beer is the king of drinks and it can be found, drunk and enjoyed in nearly every country of the world.

Beer is the oldest known alcoholic drink and dates from before 4000 BC when it was first brewed in Mesopotamia and in Egypt where that land's ancients gave it a hieroglyph. But the modern brewing industry has sixteenth-century origins and they are mainly in Europe.

Here the world's finest beers in present day culture can be found in a band that stretches from Austria and the Czech Republic through Germany, Denmark and the Low Countries and across the North Sea to the British Isles.

It is significant however that the United States, China and Japan now take their place with Germany as the top four brewing nations in the world although it is the Czechs and the Germans who are the world's greatest drinkers.

The International Book of Beer takes you on a journey around the breweries of the world, stopping off for a while at those where the great beers are brewed and meeting some of the people who brew them. We will also learn about some unique and interesting beers; some of which we may never drink or even want to drink, and others that we may yearn for passionately.

A SHORT HISTORY OF BEER

The birth of brewing came a little too early to be well chronicled and the best guess as to when the first beer was made, and drunk, is around 4000 BC, or maybe a century or two earlier, in the Bible lands of Mesopotamia and Egypt.

The process almost certainly came about by accident with some damp grain turning itself into malt and fermentation developing naturally. Even today in Belgium one style of beer is made by the spontaneous fermentation of wild yeasts.

The histories of bread and ale are interlinked as they use much the same raw materials and the English poet John Taylor called beer 'a loaf out of a brewer's basket'. And although methods of brewing have changed over the years the essential process remains much the same today.

In medieval Europe the monks were the principal brewers of ale, then a sweet and glutinous drink. It was regarded as a food and an important part of the diet. Reports of several quarts a day being consumed in the monasteries are not as outrageous as they seem. Not only was ale a food but because it had been boiled it was considerably safer to drink than water.

But this was ale; beer needed something extra and that was hops which not only added extra flavour but also acted as a preservative. There are records of hops being used for brewing in Central Europe from the ninth century but it was not until the fifteenth century that they reached Britain. From then on a clear distinction could be drawn between ale and beer.

Nowadays the difference is less finely drawn and the terms ale and beer are almost synonymous. Beer is a useful umbrella word and ale can be distinguished from such styles as lager and stout. And for all of them hops are necessary; an essential to provide flavour and to act as a preservative.

The establishment of 'common' brewers whose job it was to provide beer for all: inn or tavern, farm, stately home or private house, was well established in Britain by 1700 but in other nations the small village brewer remained the norm. In Bavaria there are still more than 800 breweries of which only ten can be called large. Nearly every village has at least one brewery.

The great names of the brewing world can be traced from the last century except in Britain where Whitbread, Bass and Guinness were internationally known by the year 1800. Then

The Brewer, Jan Luyken (1649–1712)

along came such firms as Carlsberg of Denmark, Heineken of the Netherlands and Pilsner in Bohemia with Anheuser-Busch in the United States following later.

Although the technology of brewing has developed particularly in the present century, it is in the last twenty-five years that

Flemish Tavern, Adriaen van Ostade
(1610–1685)

The Happy Drinker, Judith Layster (1609–1660)

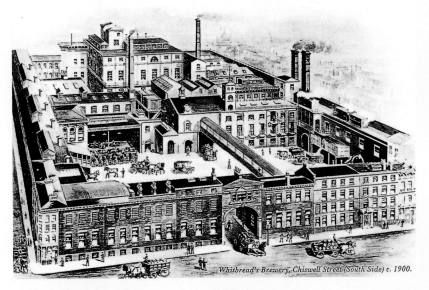

Whitbread's Brewery, Chiswell Street (South Side) c. 1900.

Whitbread's brewery c.1900 (Whitbread Archive)

Hops are added to the brew in traditional coppers at the Eldridge Pope brewery, Dorchester, England

Strathcona Community Centre
601 Keefer Street
Vancouver, BC V6A 3V8
(604) 713-1838
Registration Receipt

| Date: 04/15/2001 | Receipt #: 410014110 | User ID: 008 | Site: 01 |

PAYEE INFORMATION

Wei (Jessica) Yeoh
7550 Aubrey Street
Burnaby, BC V5A 1K7

Customer #: 006491
299-4757 (604)   -   (604)

PAYMENT INFORMATION

Amount Charged	$ 4.00
GST	$ 0.00
PST	$ 0.00
Total Amount Due	$ 4.00
Amount Paid	$ 4.00
Balance Due	$ 0.00

PAYEE ACCOUNT INFORMATION

Prior Balance	$ 0.00
Used To Pay Fees	$ 0.00
Current Balance	$ 0.00

Cash	$ 4.00	ID #:		
Cheque	$ 0.00	Cheque #:	Bank #:	
Card	$ 0.00	Card #:	Card Type:	
Memo	$ 0.00	Memo #:		

ENROLLEE(S):

AN Wei (Jessica) Yeoh	**Activity:** 0000.503 2001 Membership	**Fees:**	$ 4.00
Account 2001 Membership 0001	**Location:** No location		
From 12/01/2000 **To** 12/31/2001 F	**Times** 09:00AM 10:00PM	**Amount Applied:**	$ 4.00
		Amount Owed:	

Thank you for your payment!

Refund: All requests for refunds must be received by the Community Centre office before the start of the second class. All refunds are subject to an administrative charge.

Whitbread hop farm and oast houses, Kent, England

Tradition and technology combine at Bass's Cape Hill plant, Birmingham, England

social changes and consumer demand have had most influence on the beers of the world. Lager style beers have swept across the globe and in Britain 'real' ales have become the vogue with many small companies being formed to brew them. In the United States as well, small is beautiful with 400 micro breweries opening in this period.

The world of beer has never been more interesting. There are dozens of varying styles of beer and thousands of different brands many of which are available well away from their country of origin.

HOW BEERS ARE BREWED

In its simplest form beer is made from water (which the brewer calls 'liquor'), malt, hops and yeast. Sometimes other materials are added but the basic ingredients remain the same.

Malt, usually malted barley, is ground to a rough flour – called grist – and then mashed with hot water in a mash tun. The natural sugars from the malt are extrated and dissolve in the liquor to form what is now called the wort.

This is then boiled and hops are added in a vessel called a copper or kettle. After cooling the hopped wort is run into fermentation vessels and yeast is added. The action of this

Opposite: Cooper at work, Young's brewery, London

Above and opposite: Great British Beer
Festival, Olympia, London

converts the sugars into alcohol – in this case beer – and after
settling this is drawn off into containers – casks, kegs, cans or
bottles – for serving.

This is all very simplistic and there are many variations in both
materials and the process. Grains other than barley such as
wheat can be used and unrefined sugars can be added at the
mashing stage. Hops, which act as both a flavouring and a
preservative may be added at different stages, even after the
brewing process is complete: called 'dry-hopping'.

There are different kinds of yeast. Those for making ales and
stouts work on top of the cooled wort, whereas bottom fermenting yeasts are used for lagers and act at much lower temperatures and usually for longer periods.

Beer at its best remains a living thing; 'real ale' brewed in
Britain is the classic example of this. At the other end of the
scale beers are filtered and pasteurised and do not mature any
further; 'keg beer' is the most appropriate style. Between the two
is a world of beer to explore.

THE RENAISSANCE OF BEER

Just prior to this book going to print a new beer went on sale in
many English pubs. It was from the Bateman family brewery on
the Lincolnshire coast and it is called Strawberryfields. Locally
grown fruit had been added to the wort just before cooling for
fermentation. The result was an unusual bitter beer with a very
slightly sour taste, hints of strawberries in the flavour and a
wonderful aroma.

There is nothing new about beers with fruit flavours; the
Belgians have been making them for centuries. But here was a
brewer not only using an unusual fruit and not macerating it for
months as a Belgian brewer would do but adding it at the stage
when many brewers add aroma hops. And it worked.

Twenty-five years ago no English brewer would have dared to
do what Martin Cullimore of Bateman's brewery did. He would
have been derided for his intemperate action. But then, twenty-
five years ago good beers were vanishing – with some honourable exceptions.

In Britain traditional ales were being phased out by the 'big six' brewers, who controlled eighty per cent of the market, and being replaced by keg beers. In the United States pale, not very strong lagers were moving towards being the only beers available. In Germany local styles of beer were just that, local, and elsewhere it was the ubiquitous lager. And in other nations it was the same. The turn of the century or even much earlier was being marked as the day when we would all drink Universal Megakeg, a fizzy, cold, bland, ersatz lager.

And then along came CAMRA – the Campaign for Real Ale – in Britain. Within five years this articulate, boistrous, impertinent, hard working group of mainly young people turned the market round. They not only stopped the move away from traditional 'real' ale but reversed the trend and saw more than two hundred new breweries built in Britain – all dedicated to the cause of real ale. CAMRA also persuaded the 'big six' brewers to move back to their roots.

The drinkers of The Netherlands followed suit and an organisation called PINT (possibly aping the word pint, the popular British measure for a drink of beer) was formed. The fight was on against uniformity.

In the United States it was the highly developed organisation of home brewers who started the move back. There was no organised campaign; no attack on the mega-brewers. What happened was that many home brewers confident of their ability to make beers that would be appreciated by a wider audience opened up small breweries or started up beer cafeAC and brew pubs. The movement multiplied and in twenty years forty breweries became four hundred. The renaissance of good beer was here.

The brew pub phenomena spread across the world; into Austria, Australia, South Africa, Canada, France, Hungary and now more lately into Russia. There are even some in Germany where most towns still have their own local breweries. In Britain they have grown like topsy, as part of the real ale revolution. Even the 'big six' breweries opened some of their own. Never before in history have there been as many beer styles as there are today. Older, more established, beers have been developed and speciality beers are now recognised across the world, copied, re-established and given further development. It is an exciting period for beer. Blandness is out, flavour is in. Pass me a pint of Bateman's Strawberryfields please.

Single Stout, Cobbs label c.1900

BEER STYLES AROUND THE WORLD

Barley Wine: By implication a beer as strong as wine which some are. Most have a strength of more than 8% abv and are rich and sweet and often very dark.

Bitter: A term which is usually applied to a draught that is

Old beers

relatively highly hopped and although its strength can vary from 3.5% to 5.5% it is in the lower range that most bitters will be found.

Bock or Bok: Often simply the German for a strong beer. It may also qualify another style of beer such as a Weizenbock (qv).

Bottle Conditioned Beers: This is not a style of beer but a treatment of beers which are not pasteurised or filtered and when bottled have yeast and sugar added to start a secondary fermentation.

Brown Ale: Almost always found in a bottle. In Britain there are two versions. The one on most brewery lists is a sweet, dark and inoffensive beer of low gravity but in the north-east of England it is stronger, more flavourful and held in great esteem. In Belgium it is a different style entirely being much more assertive.

Export: A style of beer brewed in the German city of Dortmund, pale and dry and relatively strong. Elsewhere it refers to a premium beer, usually bitter in style with a strength of around 5% which is unlikely to be for export.

Lager and Pilsner: Lager is the German word for 'store'. This style of beer was invented in Vienna in 1840 and soon became popular in Bavaria and Bohemia from where some of the classic contemporary lagers and pilsners (which is a style of lager) came. The system of brewing differs from ale brewing mainly in the use of a bottom fermenting yeast and long fermentation

Bottle conditioned beers go through a secondary fermentatiion in the bottle

periods at low temperatures – hence 'store'.

Lambic and Gueuze: Lambic beers are produced by spontaneous fermentation and are unique to a small area to the east of Brussels. Gueuze is a blend of Lambic beers. The addition of cherries which are allowed to macerate produces a Kriek and raspberries a Frambozen or Framboise.

Marzen: A medium strength beer brewed in Germany for the Autumn festivals. It takes its name from the time when it was brewed in March and stored in cool cellars or caves and drunk during the summer when brewing was not possible.

Mild: Mainly found in Britain and generally relating to a low gravity, lightly hopped beer that is usually dark brown and rather sweet.

Old Ale: Old ales should be medium to strong beers, usually dark and of great character. Many of them are only brewed in winter. Not all beers that use the prefix 'old' fit into this style, being neither old nor strong.

Pale Ale: A mid-strength, highly hopped bottled beer, often called India Pale Ale which historically was brewed to withstand the long sea voyage from Britain to India. The style is closely associated with Burton upon Trent one of England's major brewing centres. Nowadays the term is often debased and used for ordinary draught bitters.

Rauchbier: Bottom-fermented beers produced mainly in the Bamberg area of Northern Bavaria by the use of smoked malts.

Scotch Ale: Strong dark beers with a definite malt accent in the Scottish manner. They are very popular in Belgium and some brands are brewed in Scotland exclusively for export.

Stout and Porter: In the eighteenth century Porter was the most popular beer in England but it lost out to the pale ales developed at Burton upon Trent and almost vanished from the brewing scene. It was dark, rich and very hoppy and the standard drink of the porters of the London markets. Stout

Gueuze, a blend of Lambic beers from east of Brussels in Belgium

developed as a 'stouter' form of porter and its greatest protagonist was Arthur Guinness of Dublin. It was greater in strength and body than porter.

Trappist and Abbey Beers: The monks of the five Trappist breweries of Belgium (and one in The Netherlands) have their beer style protected by law. They are strong, rich, bottled-conditioned beers. Abbey beers ape the style although most of them are not brewed in an Abbey.

Weissebier or Weizenbier: The German style of white or wheat beers in which large amounts of wheat are used in the brew. They can be light or dark and a Dunkel Weizen is not a contrdiction, it means a dark wheat beer. Berliner Weisse is a separate style; highly carbonated and of lesser strength.

White beer or Witbier: The Belgium style of wheat beer which is often flavoured with spices and herbs. It can often now be found in the United States and occasionally in Britain.

NOTE ON THE STRENGTH OF BEERS

The strength of beers can be measured in several different ways, often related to the way in which taxation and duty is levied in a particular country. However a universal system does appear to be emerging where the alcohol in a beer is measured according to its volume. Alcohol by volume or abv is the system used in this book.

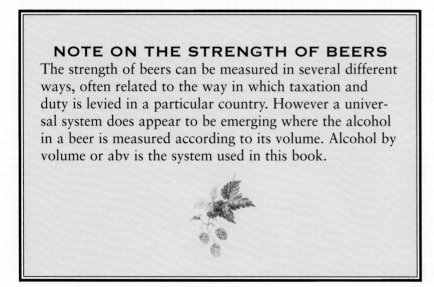

COUNTRY BY COUNTRY GUIDE

GREAT BRITAIN AND IRELAND

Great Britain is the only nation in the world to preserve the original style of brewing known as cask conditioned or real ale. There was a time, some twenty-five years ago, when it looked as if this would vanish. In an attempt to make brewing and serving beer easier the move to keg and bright beers particularly by the large national brewers gathered momentum and these blander, less interesting, beers looked set to take over.

However, consumer organisations such as the Campaign for Real Ale (CAMRA) fought off the challenge and real ale was not only saved but has since prospered. Brewing in Britain has a distinguished history and supports many different styles. It is also self- sufficient with excellent barley for malting and hops being grown there.

The five largest brewing companies – Allied, Bass, Courage, Scottish and Newcastle and Whitbread – dominate the market and a group of fifty or so regional and mainly independent brewers take a smaller but substantial share. Some two hundred small, micro and pub breweries make up the rest of Britain's

Black Sheep brewery, Masham

Opposite: The Burton Union system of fermentation, Marstens brewery, Burton upon Trent

Yorkshire square fermenting vessel, producing alcohol and carbon dioxide

beer production. Bitters, premium strength beers, mild ales, pale ales, old and strong ales and porters and stouts along with some regional variations make up the list for British beer which can lay claim to be amongst the finest in the world.

In Scotland the names of the styles often differ from those in England and Wales and in the Republic of Ireland the principal beer is dry stout although small amounts of ale and lager are also produced both there and in Northern Ireland.

BITTER – THE POPULAR BREW

Every brewery brews a standard bitter. This is usually a beer with a strength of between 3.5% and 4.0% alcohol by volume (abv) and a good hop rate. They are easy to drink and often called 'session' beers. It is by far the most popular style of beer in Britain.

The top selling bitter in Britain – and probably the world! – is a refreshingly smooth ale brewed in Leeds, West Yorkshire, by the Joshua Tetley brewery which is part of the Allied group.

Another big seller also brewed in Yorkshire is Courage's malty John Smith's Bitter from Tadcaster, a small town that supports three breweries. Next door to John Smith's is Samuel Smith's brewery – John was the father, Samuel the son. 'Sams' remains fiercely independent and is still under family control. It produces Old Brewery Bitter, a rich malty brew.

Beers from the north of England dominate the bitter market in volume terms. Boddington of Manchester which is part of the Whitbread empire, produces a pale, creamy bitter which is widely advertised and sells across England. Another big seller is the Scottish and Newcastle group's Theakston Best Bitter with its delicate hoppy flavour. It is brewed both in Newcastle and in its original home town of Masham in North Yorkshire.

There are two breweries in the small market town of Masham with connections to the Theakston family. The original T & R

Drayhorses from the Tetley brewers in Leeds, Yorkshire, an increasingly rare sight

Theakston brewery dates back to 1827 while the Black Sheep Brewery was set up in 1992 by Paul Theakston, a great grandson of the founder, after the family firm was taken over by Scottish and Newcastle. It brews a dry hoppy Black Sheep Bitter and a stronger Black Sheep Special.

Some of the finest bitters in England are made by the regional independent breweries. These include Bateman's XB from Lincolnshire, Eldridge Pope's Dorchester Bitter, Everard of

29

The drayhorse tradition still runs true at Youngs, London

Leicester brew Beacon Bitter and then there are those from the London breweries: Young's Bitter and Fuller Smith and Turner's Chiswick Bitter. All are excellent with their own distinct flavours and are mainly related to their own localities.

The small independent brewers with their micro breweries many of which turn out no more than 100 barrels each week produce some excellent examples of bitters. Butterknowle brewery in County Durham has a hoppy full flavoured Bitter; there is the copper- coloured Uley Bitter from Gloucestershire; Franklin's Bitter from Harrogate in North Yorkshire is aromatic – 'smells like a bunch of fresh flowers' – and close by in the same town the Rooster brewery sends out a series of bitters according to the season. Wherry Best Bitter from the Woodforde brewery near Norwich has won several awards.

Another range of Bitters are the rather stronger Premium beers which have a strength of between 4.0% and 4.5% abv. Landlord from the small Timothy Taylor brewery at Keighley in West Yorkshire, a wonderfully tasting aromatic ale, is amongst the best known. It was Champion Beer of Britain in 1994. Others include Brain's S A Best Bitter from Cardiff (known locally as 'Skull Attack), Greene King Abbot Ale from Suffolk, McMullen's Country Best Bitter from Hertford and from Devizes in Wiltshire, Wadworth 6X. The use of Xs to indicate strength is

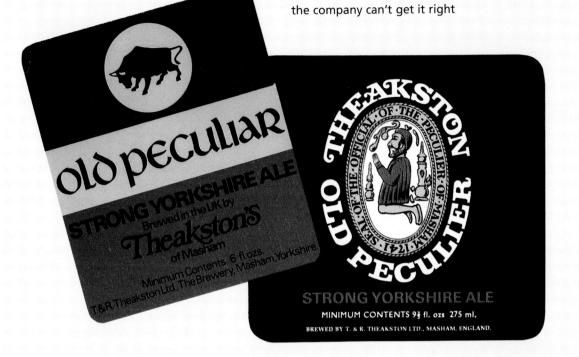

Old peculiar or Old Peculier? Sometimes even the company can't get it right

A traditional tower brewery – Ward's of Sheffield

The Queen Mother pulls herself a pint of Young's Special, although it is doubtful she actually drank it!

an ancient device although there is no coordinating link between breweries – one's 6X may be another's 4X.

From the micro breweries come some excellent examples of the genre: Exmoor Gold, a malty brew from Exmoor Ales in Somerset; Centurion Best Bitter, a well balanced brew from the Hadrian brewery in Newcastle-upon-Tyne; and Summer Lightning from the Hop Back brewery in Wiltshire is fresh, very bitter and all too easy to drink.

In Scotland the 'shilling' system is sometimes used to indicate the strength and style of beers and was once related in a complicated sort of way to its price. An Eighty shilling (80/-) beer is similar to a premium bitter (or even slightly stronger) and may also be known as an Export.

Belhaven brewery at Dunbar in the Lothians produce a light and hoppy 70/- Ale, rather unusual beer for its style for most Scottish beers are malty and rather sweet tasting. More to the

Opposite: Newcastle Brown Ale, a classic beer from the Northeast of England, now sells particularly well in the USA

Fuller's Hock, a cask conditioned mild beer from London

style are the Caledonian Brewing Company's 80/- Ale which is rich and malty and Younger No 3 a rich, dark yet dry ale. Both are brewed in Edinburgh.

MILD ALE – THE ONE TIME FAVOURITE

Mild beers are not as strong as bitters and have a lower hop rate. They are often dark but not exclusively so and in recent years have slipped back in popularity. In the last century mild

Opposite: Wells Bombardier, a fine premium bitter beer

A commemorative brew label from Okell of the Isle of Man

ales were most brewer's best seller.

Breweries in the Midlands continue to produce some outstanding examples of the style. Banks's Mild from Wolverhampton is superbly crafted with a full malt taste, Holden's Mild from Dudley is rich and fruity and Ansell's Mild from Burton upon Trent is dark, sweet and malty. A Bass outlet in Walsall brews the dry and smooth Highgate Dark which is now selling well beyond its pale.

Other areas have some distinctive mild ales. Manchester is proud of its mild heritage with established breweries such as

The Mortal Man, Troutbeck, Cumbria, has a stylish old sign framed in wrought iron

Joseph Holt, Frederic Robinson, Hyde's Anvil and John Willy Lees all retaining loyal drinkers.

On both sides of the Pennine chain of hills mild is actively promoted by both large and small brewers. In Lancashire the Best Mild of Daniel Thwaites in Blackburn and the Black Cat Mild from the nearby Moorhouse's Brewery at Burnley are both dark and full tasting.

Across the hills in Yorkshire, small breweries such as Ryburn in Sowerby Bridge, Linfit (a pub brewery) at Linthwaite near Huddersfield and Old Mill at Snaith all produce excellent milds. Further south the Nottinghamshire Mansfield brewery is noted for its Riding Mild. And whilst the famous bottles of Newcastle Brown retain their popularity in that great city they now sell better in the United States than in Britain.

In Scotland McClay's of Alloa brew a 60/- Ale that is confusingly known as 'Light' although it is very dark like an English mild. The term 'Light' indicates its strength.

PALE ALES AND OLD ALES

The historic name of Pale Ale is often used these days as an alternative for bitter but its real style is iconoclastic and relates to a heavily hopped medium strength beer closely associated with Burton upon Trent, Britain's best known brewing town.

In the early nineteenth century pale ales were shipped to India for the British troops stationed there and the term India Pale Ale (IPA) was created. The high hop rate ensured the long life necessary for the sea journey.

Many famous brewing names were established in Burton and three remain, all with a pale ale in their portfolio. Draught Bass, Ind Coope Burton Ale and Marston's Pedigree are all excellent beers and all have a distinctive sulphur nose which is known locally as 'the Burton snatch'. The famous local fermentation system known as the Burton Union is now used only by Marston's brewery.

Adnams of Southwold in Suffolk brew a range of Burton style beers and their Extra took the 1993 Champion Beer of Britain award. Fuller's of Chiswick in West London have recently introduced a very hoppy IPA based on a nineteenth-century recipe.

Bass at its brewery at Cape Hill in Birmingham produce the best known bottle-conditioned pale ale: Worthington White Shield at 5.6% abv is dry, hoppy and fruity.

The use of the term 'Old' often as a prefix for a beer is also confusing with many beers being neither old nor strong which the name indictes. But many do fit the style of rich, strong beers often called barley wines – intended to mean a beer which is as strong as a wine.

The small Hampshire brewery of Ringwood won the Champion Beer of Britain award in 1988 with its sweet, fruity 5.8% abv Old Thumper. Others which meet the style include Old Tom from Robinson's of Stockport, Owd Roger from Marston's of Burton upon Trent and the enigmatically spelled Old Peculier from Theakston of Masham which has ancient ecclesiastical origins.

GUINNESS

FOR STRENGTH

Above and opposite: Guinness advertising posters such as these are justly famous for their sparkling originality

There are also some classic bottled conditioned old ales such as Gale's Prize Old Ale (9.00%) which is corked as a wine bottle and Thomas Hardy Ale (12.00%) from Eldridge Pope which continue to develop and improve after bottling for as long as twenty-five years, maybe even longer.

STOUTER THAN A PORTER

Stouts and Porters are really London Styles of beer although little is brewed there presently. Sweeter stouts are still found in England with such well known examples as Mackeson, brewed by Whitbread and Jubilee by Bass.

The two Smith breweries in Tadcaster each produce an Imperial stout, a style that is strong, rich and meaty. John Smith's Courage Imperial Russian Stout (10.0%) was originally brewed for the Russian Court. In addition to Samuel Smith's Imperial Stout (7.0%) the brewery also produces an Oatmeal Stout (5.0%) which is a revival of an old style.

Porters pre-date stouts (a stouter drink) and take their name from the popularity of this drink with the porters of the London markets. The first ones were brewed in London in the early eighteenth century. Good modern day examples are Blunderbus from

Lovely day for a GUINNESS

the small Coach House brewery in Cheshire which has won many awards and was runner-up to the Champion Beer of Britain in 1994; Pickwick Porter from the tiny Malton brewery in North Yorkshire, another prize winner; and Blackdown Porter from Eldridge Pope of Dorchester.

THE IRISH EXPERIENCE

However, Ireland is now the natural home of dry stouts. The most famous is Guinness which can be found worldwide. The company has breweries in Dublin and London and four tropical countries and allows its beers to be brewed under licence in several others.

The firm is famous for its advertising with the use of slogans such as 'My goodness my Guinness' and 'Guinness is good for you' and some highly amusing cartoon advertisements by H M Bateman and John Gilroy.

Draught Guinness (4.2% abv) is the country's most popular drink and is found in nearly every pub in the Republic of Ireland and Northern Ireland. It is dry and bitter yet very smooth. The bottled Foreign Extra Stout (7.5%) which sells in fifty-five countries is a powerful brew, with an oaky flavour and a dry finish.

Above: Caffrey's Irish Ale sells as well in Britain as it does in Ireland

Cork, the Republic of Ireland's second city, has two stout breweries: Murphy now owned by Heineken, and Beamish and Crawford which now belongs to the Australian brewers, Foster and is therefore linked with Courage in Britain. Both are good examples of the style but not as assertive as Guinness.

At Kilkenny the Smithwick brewery, a subsidiary of the Guinness group produces a 5.4% ruby ale which sells as Smithwick's in Ireland and as Kilkenny Irish Ale in several European countries including Britain. Guinness also has ale and lager breweries in Waterford and Dundalk. Guinness brews a stronger bottled stout for Belgium which is not readily available in either Ireland or Britain and only then in the specialist beer shops which have to import it from Belgium.

Right: Guinness beer mat for Gaelic speaking areas of Ireland

A similar irony applies to some strong Scottish ales produced by Scottish and Newcastle Breweries for the Belgium trade.

Bass's Ulster brewery in Belfast produces a range of beers and lagers including a number for other brewers. Bass Ale is the top seller but the recently introduced Caffrey's Irish Ale (4.8%), a smooth caramel-tasting brew, has been an instant sales success in all parts of Great Britain.

Imports of real ale into Northern Ireland from mainland Britain are proving a success and give support to the province's only independent Hilden brewery at Lisburn in County Antrim. Ironically, up to 1995 most of its output was exported to Britain.

Pouring a pint of Irish stout is a skilled art and can take up to three or four minutes to accomplish. Experienced bar staff in Dublin pubs often sign off their handiwork by tracing a harp or shamrock in the froth on the top of the pint.

Murphy's Stout from Ireland is a firm bodied drink with a roasty style

Above: Label from Smithwick's of Kilkenny, Ireland from the days when licensees bottled their own beers

Left: Heather Ale, a recreation of an ancient brew

WESTERN EUROPE AND THE MEDITERRANEAN

BREWED AND BOTTLED BY
SIMONDS·FARSONS·CISK LTD
MALTA

CISK EXPORT Lager

Above: Cisk, Malta, an export lager with ingredients from Denmark, Germany, Belgium and Yugoslavia

Right: Pelican beer from the Pelforth brewery, Lille, France

It is easy to divide Europe into three bands of drinking cultures. In the north from Russia across Scandinavia into Scotland read 'spirits': vodka, aquavit and whisky. The middle band heading north-west from the Czech Republic through Germany and the Low Countries into the British Isles is beer country. And the southern nations are for wine. But these mainly Mediterranean bordering countries – from Portugal to Greece and into the near east have a certain amount of beer heritage and relatively thriving brewing industries.

There is a natural association between warm countries and cool lagers, although it is not always so clearly defined. Take the massive output of locally brewed Guinness stouts in Africa, the Far East and the Caribbean. But lagers hold sway in southern Europe with some small pockets of interesting and different styles of beer.

FRANCE: WHERE BEER TAKES ON WINE

Take France where the wine industry is so important to the nation's economy: Four groups dominate the brewing scene, two of which carry massive foreign investment. But in the Pas de Calais region bordering on Belgium there is an important group of small brewers producing some excellent beers known as bieres de garde.

They are top fermented ales matured at cellar temperatures for several months and often bottled with sedimentary yeast and then corked and racked. The French word 'garde' can be interpreted as 'laid down' and is similar in meaning in brewing terms to the German word 'lager' or store. They are sweetish beers though less malty than British ales and usually around a strength of 6.5%.

The Brasserie Castelain at Benifontaine produces a range of three bieres de garde under the name of Ch'ti, a slang word for northerner. The

malts used affect the colour and flavour although the strengths are much the same. Blond, Amber and Brown are joined by a weaker beer called Jade which claims to be the only organic beer in France.

Another excellent example of the genre is the smooth, tart Trois Monts from St Sylvestre close to the Belgium border. Also in border country – an area incidentally where customs posts appear not to exist – is the family run Annoeullin brewery which not only produces a *bière de garde* called Pastor Ale but also a wheat beer: L'Angelus, which is bottled in champagne style and called appropriately a *bière* de froment.

Further south in bi-lingual Alsace around the international city of Strasbourg a handful of breweries including some from the country's largest groups produce lagers in the German style although they are generally somewhat lighter in strength and colour and are identified as Biere d'Alsace.

The Pecheur brewery (which in a lingual twist markets its beers as Fischer) sell a range of stylish beers. The bottles are attractive and the beers include a dark brown beer, Adelscott, which uses whisky malt, and Fischer Gold and Fischer Tradition both of which attract national attention.

Kronenbourg, which dates from 1664, is the country's largest brewer with a massive plant in a Strasbourg suburb and another at Obernai. It is part of the food giant B S N which also, owns the Kanterbrau breweries in Lorraine and Britanny. The main selling beers which are widely exported are Kronenbourg Lager (4.7%) and the Kronenbourg 1664 light and dark beers at 6.0% abv. In the same mould as 1664 is Kanterbrau Gold which is marketed as a bière de luxe.

Left: Ch'ti bière de garde, Castelaine brewery, Béneifontaine, France

Below: Les Brasseurs beer café, Lille, France

L' Angelus bière de froment

The Dutch giant Heineken (number two in the world) also has a major stake in French brewing and owns a brewery in the small Alsace town of Schiltigheim. It is one of four breweries in the town which provide work for more than 2000 folk. Its popularity as a brewing town is because of the deep lagering cellars there that are free from the flooding which affects the area.

Heineken also own the Pelforth brewery situated near Lille. Unlike the usual *bière de garde* style of the area it produces a range of lagers, brown ales, porters and even a top fermenting all-malt beer called George Killian's Irish Red Ale (6.5%). From the middle of the last century until 1947 the original of this beer was brewed by Letts of Enniscorthy in County Wicklow in the Republic of Ireland.

It is now brewed under contract by Pelforth, for while Letts no longer brew the firm is still in business as a drinks wholesaler and claims its royalties. Heineken also brew a similar beer in The Netherlands under the name of Kylian. In the United States Coors also have a contract with Letts and George Killian's Ale brewed in Golden, Colorado, sells across the country.

SPAIN AND PORTUGAL – FOREIGN INFLUENCE

The folk of the Iberian peninsula are basic drinkers. Pale lagers are the beers for them. There are a few exceptions including some stronger lagers often called extra or premium and the occasional dark beer. The influences of other countries are there for all to see not only in the origins of the breweries but in their ownership.

Only one of Spain's major brewing groups is still in Spanish hands and that one, Damm, displays its Germanic origins by continuing to use gothic script on its labels and to call its range of beers Voll-Damm. There are breweries at Barcelona and in three other cities spread across the country.

El Aguila (The Eagle) brewery has a similar background and it produces some beers under the Adlerbrau (Eagle brew) as well as using a double eagle coat of arms reminiscent of the Austro-Hungarian empire. Aguila is now Spain's largest brewing concern having toppled San Miguel from that position after many years. Based in Madrid it is wholly owned by the Dutch Heineken brewing group.

Beers from Spain, where the brewing tradition goes back to the sixteenth century

San Miguel, which had its origins in the Phillipines continues to retain that association and the original continues to brew in Manila. In Spain there are four breweries including one in Madrid. Its beers are stronger than most of its rivals and can be found abroad. B S N of France has a stake in San Miguel and also owns one third of the Mahou brewery in Madrid. Carlsberg of Denmark has a share of the Cruz del Campo brewery in Seville.

Portugal's industry is rather insular although the popularity of beer has grown considerably in recent years. Two groups share most of the market. In Lisbon, Central de Cervejas produces the Sagres pale and dark lagers and was the first brewery to name a beer Europa – a slightly stronger pale lager than Sagres – when the country joined the European Union.

The Unicer brewery operates from Oporto and from two other modern plants built to meet the increasing demand. It has a working arrangement with Carlsberg of Denmark. There is a small brewery – Empresa – on the island of Maderia.

ASSORTED BREWS
FROM THE MEDITERRANEAN

Malta has a small but thriving brewery called Simonds-Farsons-Cisk but known locally as Farsons. It brews top fermenting beers including a pale ale, Hopleaf; a milk stout called Lacto Milk; and Blue Label Ale which is similar to an English mild in style. Imported English hops and barley are used to brew Farsons ales.

On the island of Cyprus there are two breweries: a locally

Far Right: Efes Pilsener from Turkey is brewed both in Istanbul and Izmir

Right: Keo beer, Cyprus

owned one in Limassol produces Keo lager, and Carlsberg of Denmark brew in Nicosia. Carlsberg also has a brewery in Greece as do Heineken and Lowenbrau of Munich. Little else but lager beers are produced here. Up to recently Greece had a beer purity law similar to Germany's Reinheitsgebot. The dropping of this will do little for the quality of beers brewed in Greece.

There are several breweries in Turkey of local consequence but Efes in Ankara is the largest and best known producer. In Israel where the Macabee company – a subsidiary of Canada's Labatt – produces a range of kosher beers in accordance with the Mosaic law.

Italy was until recently bottom of Europe's beer consumption table. However, an interest, particularly in specialist beers, has developed which has led to an upsurge in imports and for local breweries to try their hands at beers different to the ubiquitous lagers. Much of the present day industry is in foreign hands with Moretti of Udine owned by Labatt and Dreher (after the Austrian who invented lager in 1840) of Milan and Messina by Heineken.

Moretti brew a rich, ruby beer called La Rossa (7.5%) made with all malt and Dreher's speciality is McFarland which is made in the Scottish style but has Viennese connections!

The country's largest brewery is Peroni, with breweries in Rome and Naples and three other cities. Its products are mainly light pilsner lagers of which the best known is the widely exported Nastro Azzurro.

Below right: Two beers from Italy, which has the fastest growing consumption in Europe

SWITZERLAND – THE WORLD'S STRONGEST BEER

The Swiss not only claim to brew the world's strongest beer but they were the first country to market alcohol-free beers! There are some independent brewers in Switzerland but they tend to keep to their own areas as a consequence of anti-competition laws which at one time held that breweries could only sell within their own cantons (provinces). Three groups now operate on a national level although two of them have joined forces recently.

Feldschlosschen (castle in a field) has its main brewery and headquarters at Rheinfelden near Basel and there are five other breweries in the group. Hopfenperle, a pale lager of the style most liked by Swiss drinkers, is the group's best seller. Associated with this is the darker Dunkleperle.

Five breweries merged in 1970 to form Sibra-Holding in which the largest – Cardinal – snuffed out the others to market beers under its own name although brewing continues at all five plants. Cardinal Lager and Spezial are both produced in blond and dark versions. Feldschlosschen joined forces with Sibra in 1992 shortly after it had reached a trading

Samichlaus from Hürlimann of Zurich, Switzerland. A claimant for the world's strongest beer

Hürlimann brewery, where Samichlaus is brewed only once a year, on December 6, to be drunk the following year after the same date

Drayhorses at the Hürlimann brewery

agreement with the French brewers, Kronenbourg.

The third, and still Swiss owned, large grouping is Hürlimann of Zurich which owns another brewery in the city called Lowenbrau which has no connection with the German giant. Lowenbrau – Lion brewery – is a fairly common name throughout the world in whatever language; there are two in England.

Hürlimann brew Samichlaus (Santa Claus) which has claims to be the strongest beer in the world at 14.0% abv. On the label it says: Das starkste Bier der Welt which is then given the authority of the *Guinness Book of Records*.

There are claims against this from a German brewery (EKU at Kulmbach) and in Britain.

The beer is bottom-fermented in the lager style but that is where the similarities end. Selected strains of yeast are used to achieve this high strength and the beer takes a year to maturity. It is brewed on December 6th when St Nicholas's day is celebrated in Switzerland, and is not released into the trade until one year later.

It tastes predictably strong, yet is dry and certainly not cloying as might be expected. It is not a beer to drink in quantities. The well-known British beer writer, Michael Jackson, says it should be served from the neck of a St Bernard dog on mountain rescue duty!

THE LOW COUNTRIES AND SCANDINAVIA

Belgium has the widest variety of beer styles in the world. Many are unique, some are even regarded as bizarre, but they include some of the world's finest and in recent years have been much copied by other nations including Britain and the United States.

Some of these styles date back many centuries and have simplistic beginnings not based on the today's accepted technology of brewing. Spontaneous fermentation for Lambic beers and the uses of fruits and spices for flavouring these and other beers have no place in the modern high-tech systems but remain fixed in the popular culture of Belgium brewing.

The Netherlands, as one of the great maritime nations of the world, is a major exporter of beers. Not only in the bulk move-

Belgian Kriek (Cherry) beers

Above: Belgian Abbey beers, a range of fruity, strong ales

Opposite: Sampling beers at the Cantillon brewery, Brussels

ment of its beers to other countries – reckoned to be about half its production – but also in the technical sense with the giant Heineken brewery's involvement in around one hundred overseas breweries. The Grand Duchy of Luxembourg has a small brewing industry producing mainly German-style beers.

The most popular styles in all three of the Low Countries are Lager and Pilsner beers. They account for ninety per cent of the beer drunk in the Netherlands and, despite the variety of beers there, seventy per cent of that in Belgium.

The largest producer of lagers in the Netherlands is Heineken with two breweries in the south of the country which brew Heineken Pilsner Bier (5.0% abv) with aromas reminiscent of new-mown hay and Amstel Gold at 7.0%, which is stronger and hoppier.

Interbrew owns the two largest breweries in Belgium. From Leuven the Stella Artois Pils (5.0%) has a fresh, flowery taste and the lesser regarded hoppy Jupiler, brewed near Liege, is, nevertheless, the country's best-selling beer.

A Dutch beer which attracts attention abroad is Grolsch

Above: Grimbergen Abbey beer sign

Right: Silly scotch – from an eminently sensible brewery

Pilsner. The company has two breweries, at Groenlo and Enschede and also owns Ruddle's brewery in England. It is a fresh, sharp-tasting drink perhaps because it is unpasteurised. And one which rarely sells outside its immediate area is Christoffel Blond from the St Christoffel brewery in Roermond. It is bottled with a light sediment, tastes bitter and leaves a lasting impression.

In Belgium the Strubbe Super Pils brewed at Ichtegem near to Ostend, is another excellent small brewery product with massive hop aroma and flavours. The best known Luxembourg beer is the fresh and malty Diekirck PIls.

THE WONDERFUL 'HOLY' BEERS

Belgium and the Netherlands are noted for their 'holy' beers emanating from Trappist monasteries and abbeys. They divide into two groups with clear distinctions. The six Trappist breweries (five in Belgium, one in the Netherlands) have the name protected by law for a range of excellent ales of considerable character. The Abbey beers are all brewed in commercial breweries but are still of excellent quality.

Chimay is the largest of the Trappist breweries. It is in the south-west of Belgium and brewing began there in 1861. There are three beers whose strengths are recognised by the colour of their crown corks: Red (7.0% abv), White (8.0%) and Blue (9.0%). All are fruity in character and the Blue, which is also available in a larger, corked bottle, and known as Grande Reserve will keep and improve over several years.

Also in the south-west is the Orval monastery where just one beer is produced and then sold in a distinctive nine-pin shaped bottle. Its strength is 6.2% and it is complex and astringently bitter. The beer is very highly regarded and different from all other Trappist beers. The monks at Orval also make bread and cheese.

Another Trappist brewery in the south-west of Belgium is the smaller and lesser known Rochefort

Above: Brother Mathias at St. Sixtus Monastery brewery, Westvleteren, Belgium

Left: Duvel, a top fermenting beer from Belgium

The beers from Trappist Monastery breweries are strong and fruity

with its three distinctive beers recognised by their strength in Belgium degrees. The strongest, Rochefort 10, has an alcohol by volume strength of 11.3%. The others are Rochefort 8 and Rochefort 6. All three beers are highly respected.

The smallest of the five Belgian monastery breweries is at Westvleteren in the north-west close to the French border. The beers are not easy to find outside the specialist beer cafes and the small inn opposite the gates of the Abbey St Sixtus. Brother Mathias will welcome you at the gate of the monastery and tell you about the strong Abt (Abbot) beer at 11.55% and its lesser brothers: Extra and Special. There is also a 4.0% Dubbel brewed exclusively for the abbey – 'It's the house beer,' says Brother Mathias!

In the far north of Belgium close to the Dutch border, is the fifth of the country's Trappist breweries. The Abbey of Westmalle produces two beers – Tripel and Dubbel – in both bottled and draught form which are widely available. Like Westvleteren there is a third, weaker beer – Extra – which is brewed exclusively for the monks and brothers.

The Dutch Trappist brewery of Schaapskooi is at Koningshoeven near Tilburg in the south of the country. It is

Left: Timmermans

Above: Maltings at the Stella Artois brewery, Louvain, Belgium

Left: A group of fruit beers from Timmermans

very commercial and produces up to twelve different beers although some are not on regular sale. The best known are La Trappe Dubbel (6.5%) and La Trappe Tripel (8.0%). The most recent addition to the range is the unusual yet logically named La Trappe Quadrupel at 10.0%.

Abbey beers differ from Trappist in that they are not brewed in an abbey and although many may be licensed to do so by a religious institution that previously brewed, others may simply be in imitation of the style.

The Slagmuylder brewery, to the west of Brussels, has no

Above: Schutters

religious connections but its Abbey-style Witkap Tripel and Witkap Dubbel Pater are both excellent beers. The first uses a highly unusual technique of adding white wine to the mash.

The Van Eecke brewery at Watou in West Flanders produces a range of excellent Abbey beers under the Het Kapittel label. They include abt (10.0%), Prior (9.0%) and Pater at 8.5%.

A conventional Abbey beer comes from the Brasserie Saint Guibert to the south of Brussels. It has the contract to brew beers for the Abbaye Notre Dame de Leffre which is thirty miles away and close to Namur. Its Leffe Vielle Curvee at 8.2% is a good example of the style as is Leffe Blond (6.3%) which is widely exported in both bottled and draught form.

SPONTANEOUS FERMENTATION

Unique to Belgium are the Lambic beers of the Senne valley in the western outskirts of Brussels. Large quantities of unmalted wheat are used in the mash and fermentation is spontaneous with the brew attracting wild yeasts from the atmosphere. Further maturation takes place in large wooden barrels and can take up to three years. It is a highly complex process and the beers that emerge in various states are most unusual, often quite sour although modern tastes demand sweeter though not traditional Lambic.

Often Lambic beers are blended – young with old – which is then bottled in a way similar to champagne and called Gueuze.

Opposite: Inn sign, Amersfoort, Netherlands

Kylian – an Irish ale brewed in the Netherlands

Or they have fruits added to them; the best known version is with cherries called Kriek. Local fruit is used and is macerated in the lambic for six months during which time the beer increases in strength. A similar beer made with raspberries known as Frambozen or Framboise. Other fruits are sometimes used but there is no tradition for these.

One of the most famous Lambic brewers and Gueuze blenders is Cantillon in the Brussels suburb of Anderlecht (better known for its soccer team than for brewing.) Here amongst a range of assertive beers Rose de Gambrinus (5.0%) is a Lambic made with a mix of cherries and raspberries.

Belle Vue brewery located just out of the inner city of Brussels is highly commercial (it belongs to the multinational Interbrew) but produces some fine examples of the lambic style. Belle Vue Selection Lambic (5.2%) is an excellent blend from the 11,000 oak and chestnut casks in its cellars.

WHITE BEERS AND OTHER ENIGMAS

A style of beer that has had a renaissance in the last thirty years is white beer. It originates from the village of Hoegaarden close to Leuven. At the de Kluis brewery the best known white beer is produced, simply called Hoegaarden or in the English-speaking world to which it is widely exported, as Hoegaarden White.

The style was recreated by Pieter Celis and followed by forty other Belgium and Dutch brewers. Hoegaarden is cloudy, spicey (having coriander and orange peel added to the mash) and very refreshing.

The Netherlands and Belgium produce many other styles and brands of beers. Some are internationally known whilst others rarely move beyond their own area. Ones worth searching out

Below: La Trappe

include:
Rodenbach Grand Cru
(eighteen months old, 6.5%, red, rich
and sour), Liefmans Goudenband (5.1%, perhaps the best example of a Belgium brown ale), Brugse
Straffe Hendrik (a classic hoppy pale ale at 6.5%), Duval (8.5%
– 'Devil', strong, golden and hoppy) and any of the wonderful
range of beers from the Ij brewery on Amsterdam's waterfront.

SCANDINAVIA –
WHERE TAXES DETERMINE STRENGTH

The Scandinavian countries remain faithful to Germanic style
lagers and pilsners, mainly light coloured but with occasional
forays into darker shades. One would have expected them to be
somewhat stronger than other countries in these styles, perhaps
to protect against the fierce winters, but until recently Sweden,
Finland and Norway had restrictive laws on the gravity of beers
and heavy taxation.

In 1883 Carlsberg brewers were the first to identify and isolate a
single cell yeast culture which has left its name in the annals of
lager brewing as carlsbergensis. In 1891 the brewery was given the
seal of royal approval and one of the beers produced is Hof,

named after the royal court. This is also called Carlsberg Pilsner which is available in more than 130 countries.

Other beers include Elephant (7.7%) and the excellent though very strong Special Brew at 9.0% which is specially produced for export. Carlsberg joined with its main rival Tuborg in 1970 and together they account for eighty per cent of the Danish beer production, three-quarters of which is exported. Add to this the fact that the group own several breweries in other countries and in many more its beers are brewed under licence.

There are some independent brewers in Denmark and from these come some off-beat brews such as Bering Bryg from Ceres in Aarhus which is flavoured with lemon and rum. It is part of a group with Faxe which brews a sweet Bock in the German style. Faxe owns the Robert Cain brewery in Liverpool, England.

One obvious claim for beer in Sweden is that it is not cheap; it is probably the highest taxed in Europe. Also until quite recently there were prohibitions on the strength of both home brewed

't IJ brewery, Amsterdam

Right: Maximiliaan brewery, Amsterdam

Right and below: Labels from St. Martinus brewery, Groningen

Heineken, from the Dutch company of the same name, is probably the most widely recognised beer brand in the world

Right: Lapin Kulta, FInland

and imported beers. The strength restrictions have now been relaxed but beers remain limited by price. No one wins except the exchequer and it leaves the Swedish brewing industry with little scope for inventiveness.

The most interesting beers are exported because it is possible to sell strong beers abroad. They include Carnegie Porter brewed by Pripps of Stockholm, the country's largest brewing group and Spendrup's Old Gold which is an all malt brew and probably as strong as you can find on sale in Sweden.

Finland has a thriving industry despite punitive taxes and restrictive practices similar to those in Sweden. Any beers stronger than 4.0% abv is taxed an extra forty per cent! The biggest company is Hartwell whose Lapin Kulta is brewed at two plants in Lapland. It is a strong, at 5.3% with a clean fresh palate.

The other large brewer is Synebrichoff (Koff is the local name) which produces Brewmaster's Brown Ale and Koff Porter; both beers are dark and rich.

One beer style that is unique to Finland is sahti which is commercially brewed by small breweries but is more often made at home. It is brewed using malted barley and rye and flavoured with juniper berries.

Norway follows the German tradition in both its beers and by having a purity law similar to the Reinheitsgebot. The Rignes company is the country's largest brewer but its list of lagers contains little of character and the clutch of independent brewers have the most interesting beers.

The oldest brewery in Aass from Drammen near Oslo which dates from 1834. It is pronounced 'os' and means a summit. From its range Jule 01, a Christmas beer, and Bokk in the Bavarian style stand out.

The world's most northerly brewery is Mack in Tromso which is three hundred miles inside the Arctic circle. It has some good beers but its best known is the 4.5% Arctic Beer in a simple, refreshing lager style that sells well abroad for its curiosity value.

Iceland also exports a Polar Beer of 5.3% strength from the Olgerdin brewery in Reykjavik. Stringent laws allow beers of only 2.25% in strength to be brewed for home consumption. Icelanders in their ancient tradition must travel afar overseas to drink interesting beers.

Above: Paaske Bryg, Norway

GERMANY AND AUSTRIA

Germany ranks second amongst the world's major beer producers and its drinkers are topped only by the Czech Republic in the international beer consumption table. Forty per cent of the world's breweries are found in the now reunited country; some 1400 in total including a batch of recently opened brew-pubs.

It has many styles of beer most of which fall into geographical categories. Bavaria probably commands the most varied

The brewhouse, Löwenbräu. Munich

The Oktoberfest in Munich began in 1810 and is attended by betweenfive and six million people throughout its 16-day duration. This is the Hacker-Pschorr tent

Löwenbräu drayhorses in a festival procession

selection and the major cities of the north and west have distinguished beers which are clearly identifiable.

The Austrians are also great beer drinkers and rank fifth in the world, moving up four places in the last ten years. It is a small country with only sixty-nine breweries but there are some distinctive beer types including some created or introduced in recent years by inspirational new brewers.

Germany's place in the hierarchy of beer is due in no small part to its beer purity law – the Reinheitsgebot of 1516. This applied only to Bavaria until 1919 when that state became part of the republic and insisted on it applying to the rest of Germany. It declared that only malt, hops, yeast and water could be used in the making of beer. Although there has been a recent relaxation in respect of foreign imports most German brewers stick to the pledge and few foreign beers have made any import headway into Germany.

BEERS FROM THE NORTHERN CITIES

Hamburg is the home of Holsten one of Germany's largest brewers and the biggest exporter to Britain. Holsten Diat Pils is well attenuated with a low carbohydrate count and was originally designed for diabetics but its high alcohol (5.8%) adds too many calories to help slimmers. It is however a justifiably popular hoppy beer.

Above: German wheat beers

Left: St. Pauli Girl, Bremen

Opposite: Löwenbräu wheat beer

Above right: Dom Kölsch, Cologne

In the same city the Bavaria St Pauli brewery (which is not Bavarian) produces a range of standard lagers but its subsidiary, Jever, in the Friesland town of the same name, brews one of the world's classic beers in the pilsner style. Jever Pils (4.9%) is very dry and bitter with some wonderful malt overtones in a popular local fashion.

Bremen also has a St Pauli brewery – called St Pauli Girl – which brews both dark and light lagers with a flowery, clean flavour. But the city's best known product is Beck's Bier a fresh tasting pilsner which is widely exported in both draught and bottled form.

Further south in Münster the Pinkus Muller brewery is famous for its Pinkus Münster Alt which contains forty per cent wheat in the grist, is top fermented and is matured for six months. The result is a 5.1% abv light beer with a tart, refreshing taste.

Dortmund is the home of seven breweries all using the name 'Dortmunder'. The beer style is pale,

Right: Krombacher Pils, Kreutzal-Krombach

Top right: Zipfer, a range of hoppy beers from the Bräu AG group in Austria

Bottom Right: Puntigamer, a sweet tasting beer from Austria's Styrian breweries

dry, full bodied and usually around 5.0% abv in strength. They are usually called 'Dortmunder Export' and are protected by an appellation controlée.

The two largest breweries – DAB (Aktien) and DUB (Union) export the more popular of their products throughout Europe. Dortmunder Kronen brews an Export with a sweeter than expected taste and also Classic which is slightly stronger but in the same vogue. The Dortmunder Thier brewery which is owned by Kronen has a full-bodied Export with lots of character.

The beers of Dusseldorf are also quite distinctive. They are of a burnished copper shade, top fermented, well flavoured and clean tasting. There are four home-brew inns and four general breweries and all adopt the city's style for their standard beers, the

Ottakringer takes it name from the Vienna working class district in which it is situated

A fine example of the signmaker's art; this inn is in Vienna

Düsseldorfer Altbier. The word 'alt' meaning 'old' refers to an older style, rather than that of a beer, which has been a long time in the making.

The home-brew houses of Düsseldorf are a must for visitors with a love of beers. Three are in the old town, the other in the modern city centre. Their beers – all excellent – are simply named after the inn. In the old town look for Im Fuchschen (The Fox) which is also noted for hearty food; Zum Schlussel (The Key) and Zum Uerige which brews a wonderfully bitter beer. The Schumacher tavern is modern but for the discerning drinker there is a light, clean, aromatic beer.

The beers of Cologne also have their name protected and only those brewed in the city bounds may describe themselves as 'Kölschbier'. It is easily the most common beer in the city and often the only style to be found in its gasthofs and cafes. Kölsch is top fermented, paler than a Czech pilsner, fruity and lightly hopped with a strength of about 5.0%.

The largest producer of Kölsch is Kuppers which is also the newest commercial brewery in the city dating from 1972. It is heavily marketed and sells well outside Cologne but fails to attract local attention lacking the character of products from more well established firms.

The best known Kölsch is from Fruh's Colner Hofbrau which originated from a home brew bar in the city centre and which is still in business. Fruh Echt Kölsch is brewed from a pure barley mash which shows in the taste and is followed by a delicate hoppy finish. The Gaffel brewery produces a dry, light spicey beer whilst Muhlen Kölsch from the Malzmuhle brew cafe is again spicey and lightly hopped but distinctive; it makes an excellent aperitif.

The popular drink in Berlin is a quite distinctive white beer – Berliner Weisse – which is assertive, sharp tasting and quite low in alcohol. It takes several months to produce with a long maturation period. Up to half of the mash is malted wheat.

Weisse is served in wide bowl shaped glasses and often has raspberry or woodruff syrups added to colour the drink and take away some of its tartness. The best known, and most widely exported, example of the style is Berliner Kindl Weisse but the city's connoisseurs will opt for Schultheiss Berliner Weisse.

BAVARIANS – WORLD CHAMPION BEER DRINKERS

While Germans as a nation drink more than two hundred and fifty pints of beer each on average in a year, Bavarians leave the rest of the country standing by consuming more than four hundred pints each. This most independent of Germany's states is also the home for some seven hundred and fifty breweries, more than half of the nation's total.

Brewing as an art, craft and science is taught at the Weihenstephan brewery in Freising twenty miles north of Munich. It is the oldest brewery in the world with records dating from 1040 and is part of the Technical University of Munich. Many of the world's greatest brewers are amongst its alumni. As a commercial brewery it has a portfolio of ten beers which can best be enjoyed under the chestnut trees in the beer garden next to the brewery.

Bavaria is also the home of several distinct styles of beer including the unique smoked beers of Franconia in the north of the state and the town of Bamberg in particular. These Rauchbiers are made with barley malt that has been smoked over beech chips in the drying process and which gives a burnt flavour to the finished beers most of which have a strength of around 5.0%.

Some Rauchbiers are dark, even black, which seems appropriate to the style. Klosterbrau brews a Schwarzla which is dark brown and a complex mix of hops and smoked malt. The best-known brewery, Schlenkarla, has a Rauchbier Marzen which is coal black. The Spezial brewery's Lagerbier is light, fruity and smoked and takes its inappropriate sounding name because it is 'lagered' for several months. Lager is simply the German word for store and is not generally used to describe a beer.

Munich, the state capital, is the home of a dozen breweries including what are known as the big six: Augustiner (the oldest dating from 1328), Hacker-Pschor, Hofbrau (the former royal court brewery, now state owned), Löwenbräu (internationally known for exporting), Paulaner and Spaten.

Their entrenched position in the city is such that they are the only breweries that take part in the famous Oktoberfest. Attempts to break down this monopoly over the years have failed and it remains a money-spinner for the large breweries.

The feast started in 1810 to celebrate the wedding of Bavaria's Crown Prince. Then there was horse racing and beer drinking. Now there are also side shows, many exciting fun fair rides and still beer drinking.

The big six each host a massive tent and for sixteen days drinking, eating, carousing and singing goes on unabated. Each year more than five million litre steins of beer are consumed along with 800,000 chickens, 250,000 pairs of sausages and eighty head of beef.

Special beers are brewed for the festival although these days they are really only slightly more stronger beers than the standard pale beers of the Munich beer houses. At one time dark, strong Marzen beers were served. They were brewed in March and stored until October.

Munich is the home of Doppelbock or Starkbier which are drunk in early spring to celebrate the passing of winter. The city adapts its drinking to the seasons. They are usually as strong as 10.0% abv, even higher, and most add 'ator' to their name: Curator, Operator, Salvator, and Fortunator. The EKU brewery in Kulmbach produces Kulminator (7.5%) and the impressive Kulminator 28 with a strength of 13.5%. This vies with the Swiss beer Samichlaus to be the strongest in the world on regular sale.

Dark lagers (Dunkel) are special to Bavaria and generally have more character than lighter versions. Although they are malty they are often dry with a hoppy aftertaste. These beers were the common drink of Munich until the 1930s but are now only found in bottled form. Those worth seeking out are Bayerisch Dunkel from Ettl in Teisnach, Klosterschwarzbier brewed by Monchshof in Kulmbach and Konig Ludwig Dunkel from the Kaltenberg brewery which is at the castle of Prince Luitpold, thirty miles from Munich.

The Bavarian style of wheat beer is becoming very popular after almost dying out earlier this century. It is called Weissbier or Weizenbier and is top fermented from a mash of wheat and barley malt – roughly half and half. It may be light or dark and is usually unfiltered. Weissbier tastes tart and fruity, is heavily carbonated with a strength of about 5.5% abv. Bottled versions are reckoned to be better than draught.

Most of the major breweries produce Weissbiers but it is from some of the smaller firms that the classic products can be found. Schneider of Kelham produce Schneiderweisse (5.4%) which has a rich sharp fruity taste and a dry finish and also Aventinus (8.0%) which is dark with a sweeter approach followed by a dry finish; fruit persists throughout. Schneider has a beer cafe in the centre of Munich where stiff-aproned matrons serve you excellent beers and food albeit with little grace; it is nevertheless worth a visit.

The Pfefferbrau (Pepper brewery – no relation to the author) at Zwiesel produces an out of the ordinary beer called Dampfbier, literally 'steam beer'. There is no connection however. The beer is fruity with a touch of raspberries and similar to an English bitter ale. The Maisel brewery in Bayreuth brews a similar beer.

The most unusual beer in Bavaria is called Zoigl. It is not easy to find and is not produced in commercial quantities but often brewed by families or groups of neighbours. It belongs to an area in the north-west corner of the state close to the Czech border.

Zoigl beggars description for it varies and no two brews from the same brewery are said to be alike. Graham Lees, author of *The Good Beer Guide to Munich and Bavaria* discovered one in the village of Windisch-Eschenbach and he described it as an amber beer; rich, full-bodied with a dry finish. He advices seekers of this elusive beer to contact the local tourist office for help!

AUSTRIA – WHERE LAGER COMES FROM

According to Austria's premier beer writer, Conrad Seidl, lager was invented in Vienna in 1840. This was a year before a similar claim was made in Munich and two years prior to the creation of the Pilsner style of lager in nearby Bohemia. The man responsible for the Vienna style was Anton Dreher and it was at the Schwechat brewery a few miles to the south of the capital city.

The brewery is still in business as part of Austria's largest brewing group, Brau AG, which is based in Linz. Other breweries are in Wieselburg, Innsbruck and Zipf in the Salzburg province. From here comes Zipfer Urtyp (original Zipf) which is a sharp, hoppy beer that sells throughout the country. Another national brand is Kaiser, a fruity lager which is brewed at several plants. From Schwechat the Steffl brand is popular in Vienna – it

Beer cellar, Mayrofen, where wood chopping prowess goes hand in hand with monumental consumption!

takes its name from the city's cathedral: St Stephen's.

The other large brewing group is Stryian Breweries with two breweries in the home province of Styria and one at Lienz in the Tyrol. Gösser beers are sold nationwide; Gösser Spezial is a clean-tasting malty beer and its sister Gösser Export carries more body and a sharper flavour. Also featured in the group are the Puntigamer beers.

Vienna's only commercial brewery is Ottakringer which dates from 1837 and takes its name from the suburb in which it is located. Every year on the anniversary of its founding (September 13th) the brewery opens its gates to the good folk of Ottakring and invites them to tour the brewery, drink the beer, eat some chicken or a sausage and listen to some typically Viennese folk music. According to Engelbert Wenckheim, its managing director, it is an opportunity to repay the local folk for drinking Ottakringer beer down the years.

The best selling beers are named Gold Fassl with a 4.6% Pils and a 5.5% Spezial. Both are smooth and full of flavour. The latest addition to the range is Ottakringer Helles which at 5.1% indicates it is light in colour rather than in strength. There is also a speciality bottled beer selection under the Kapsreiter label of Hell, Goldbraun and Bock beers.

Vienna has six mini breweries producing a varied range of regular style and special beers. At Nussdorf the Baron von Echt produces the top fermenting Sir Henry's Stout and a wheat beer called Doppelhopfen Hell. In nearby Dobling Sep Fischer sells some delightful pilsners from his impressively titled Erste Wiener Gasthofbrauerei.

There is a scattering of brew pubs across Austria, all part of the renaissance of beer that has swept Europe and North America in the last two decades.At Kefermarkt in Upper Austria Wolfgang Rajal has built one in a castle and in a good ecological manner uses his spent grains from brewing to flavour his own home-baked bread.

In the same province at Eggenberg and also in a castle, McQueen's Nessie Whisky Malt Red Beer is made with Scotch Whisky Malt to a strength of 7.5%. The brewer says it tastes like a whisky and soda!

CZECH REPUBLIC AND EASTERN EUROPE

Arguably the most glorious lagers in the world come from the Czech Republic. It was here in 1842 in the city of Pilsen – now known as Plzen – that the wonderful golden-coloured beers were first brewed, hence the term and beer style, Pilsner.

The other main Czech brewing town, Ceske Budejovice (formerly known as Budweis), produces similar beers with less robust characteristics, softer and perhaps a little more sophisticated but of similar, superb quality. And the capital city of Prague with its clutch of breweries adds its weight along with the many provincial plants to the country's brewing culture; in fact nearly every town and city has its own brewery.

Staropramen (old sprig) in Prague is the Czech Republic's largest brewers

One-time lagering vessels from the Budvar brewery now used as holiday chalets in the garden of a pub in a suburb of Prague

No wonder then that the Czechs are among the world's greatest drinker's, consuming almost three hundred pints each in a year. They beat the Americans by forty pints. The Hungarians are the only other Eastern European nation to figure in the top ten of beer consumers.

The lager brewing triangle of Munich, Pilsen and Vienna contains a magnificent array of fine beers. All three cities make claims on being the 'first' and depending on what is being discussed, each is correct.

But all agree that the first successful commercially brewed bottom-fermented beers came from Munich in the 1820s – but these were dark lagers. In 1840 Vienna brought out the first lighter coloured lagers although they were of a reddish, copper hue. But it was at Pilsen in 1842 that the now much copied golden pilsner lager, one of the world's great beer styles, was created.

The Plzen brewery remains in business to this day, producing the 4.3% abv Pilsner Urquell. Urquell means 'original source'

Beers from the Czech Republic

and whilst many lesser brewers debase the word Pilsner none dare claim its uniqueness. After its first fermentation the beer is matured in underground caverns for seventy days. This produces a full bodied, bitter and complex beer of great character.

The brewery shares a site with Gambrinus, the largest brewery in the Czech Republic. It produces a 5.0% pilsner which is lighter in body and not as bitter as Urquell and not as full flavoured due to a shorter secondary fermentation.

The ready availability of Saaz (locally known as Zatec) hops from norther Bohemia is one of the great benefits the Czech brewing industry enjoys. Excellent malting quality barley is also grown locally. At Plzen they use both ingredients and their quality is obvious.

The two breweries belong to a newly formed and privatised group called Western Bohemian Breweries which also includes the Domazlice brewery close to the German border. It brews a dark lager called Purkmistr (4.7%) with an intense malt nose

Above right: Bohemia Regent

and spicey, chocolate flavours. It has much local support particularly when mixed with Gambrinus – two people will share a bottle of each – in much the same way that 'mixed', a union of mild and bitter, is drunk in some parts of England.

THE BREWING GEMS OF SOUTH BOHEMIA

The attractive south Bohemian city of Ceske Budejovice (previously known by its German name, Budweis) is the home of two breweries: the more famous Budvar and the older Samson. Close by in the town of Trebon is the Regent Brewery. All three produce excellent beers.

The most famous beer of the region is the widely exported 5.0% Budweiser Budvar. It is a smooth beer with a pleasant bitter flavour with a touch of vanilla and a fine hoppy aroma. The brewery dates from 1895, twenty years after Adolphus Busch visited the town and took back to the United States his version of the beer and its trade marked name. Legal wrangles over the years allow the Czech version to be

Right: The two Budweisers

Left: Maltings, Samson brewery, Ceské
Budejovice

sold across Europe but not in the USA. Most beer experts recognise the superiority and tradition of the Czech version.

The Samson brewery which dates from 1795 brews a range of beers under its own name. Samson Dark and Samson Light – known locally as 'people beer' – are comparatively low in strength (4.5%), they are inexpensive and account for eighty per cent of the plant's production. Higher gravity beers include Samson Gold and Samson Crystal and Zamek which is brewed for export to Britain.

Brewing in Trebon started in 1379 and the present building in a castle style dates from 1698. The principal beers are the very hoppy Bohemia Regent and the rich malty Black Regent. Both are 4.8% in strength and are exported to European countries.

CAPITAL BEERS

There are three commercial breweries in the Czech Republic's capital city all part of the Prague Breweries company in which the British brewers, Bass, have a financial stake. The largest of these, Staropramen, produces a golden, malty lager with pleasant bitterness and a strength of 4.0%. It is exported throughout Europe and to America.

The two smaller breweries in the group, Branik and Holesovice, cater mainly to the local taste. The Branik favourites are a spicey light lager and dark, characterful beer. Holesovice brews a yeasty beer called Prazan pale.

The best known beer in Prague is from the beer-tavern U Fleku which is in the area known as the New Town, even though it dates from 1499. It is a very dark lager with a touch of ruby and rich malt and toffee flavours. The Novomestsky beer-tavern in the city centre was built as recently as 1994. Here drinkers can sit amongst the brewing equipment and enjoy a well balanced refreshing pilsner.

Above Right: Pilsner
Urquell

Right: Wall painting by Josef Lada of a fight in
a beer hall at the Gambrinus brewery, Pilsen

The republic's second city, Brno, has a large brewery in which
the Austrian group Brau AG has a stake. It produces a flavourful
dark beer called Brnensky Drak (Brno Dragon).

Pardubice in central Bohemia is noted more for its famous
horse race each October than for its brewing. But the local
brewery as well as making a standard lager, every Christmas it
produces a dark bottom-fermenting porter which at 7.5% is the
strongest beer made in the republic. In Moravia the brewery at
the mining town of Ostravar makes a tasty Amber Ale at 5.0%.

The break-up of Czechoslovakia in 1992 left Slovakia as a

Left: The brew house,
Gambrinus brewery,
Pilsen

country with little brewing tradition. It was always the case that
the western provinces were for beer and the eastern – Slovakia –
for wine.

But Slovakia does have a clutch of breweries producing some
interesting beers including some in the porter style. At Martin in
central Slovakia, the Martinsky Porter weighs in at a hefty 8.0%
although it is a beer that is hard to find outside its home town.
This is the strongest beer in Slovakia and stronger than any in
the Czech Republic.

At the Zlaty brewery near Bratislava two lagers are brewed –
Bazant which is in the Pilsner style and quite hoppy; and Topvar,
a dryer, malty beer. Both are 4.5% abv in strength.

Above: Zywiec beer from Poland

AFTER THE IRON CURTAIN – BEER

The other Eastern European countries are all beer producers but mainly of standard lager style beers and few of them are of any character. There has certainly been an upsurge in brewing since the lifting of the iron curtain and western money and technical assistance is helping particularly in the setting up of brew pubs.

Centre: Zywiec beers imported into Austria

The Hungarians are great beer consumers ranking tenth in the world. But their market is concentrated with seven breweries producing ninety per cent of the output. In Budapest the Kobanyai brewery brews a range of beers

Below right: Russian beers

including K125 a 5.0% pilsner and Bak which is a 7.5% dark bok.

A number of brew-pubs have opened since 1990, mainly in Budapest. German and British money has poured in but there has been little by way of style development and most of the beers are similar to Munich lagers.

Poland has seventy breweries which cater for local taste. Two which have both a national and international reputation are

Top left: A truckload of Budweiser Budvar, from the Bohemian city of Ceske Budejovice

the Zywiec near Cracow and Tatra in the southern mountains. The Grodzisk brewery near Poznan brews a porter made with smoked malt which if not unique is certainly most unusual.

Throughout the nations of the former Soviet Union local breweries abound producing standard beers and little of interest. In Moscow Zhihuli beers are well known and some are exported. A pilsner beer from this brewery can often be found in western Europe; it is in the Czech style but not as sophisticated.

The latest development in Russia is the introduction of British type pubs to Moscow which are financed by British capital including some from breweries.

Left: The Budvar brewery
c.1900

NORTH AND SOUTH AMERICA AND THE CARIBBEAN

There is a long brewing tradition in North America, but it is only in recent years that new styles have developed, mainly as a result of the work of home brewers and the influence that foreign beer imports have had on local producers. As a result many tiny breweries have started up in the United States and Canada and some of the larger ones have moved to brew styles not seen in their portfolios for many years.

Immigrants were mainly responsible for the original styles of beers found in modern day brewing and Dutch, Czech and particularly German influences were well in evidence in the USA up to the 1919 Volstead Act and the resultant prohibition. The effect of prohibition was devastating. Between 1920 and 1980 the number of breweries fell from 4000 to less than 40. The renaissance of beer has now multiplied that number ten times.

Adolphus Busch, a young brewer of German origin living in St

Pete's Wicked Ale, brewed in St. Paul Minnesota, won the brown ale gold medal at the 1992 Great American Beer Festival

Louis, Missouri, married Lily Anheuser in 1861. She inherited her father's brewery and the foundations of the world's largest brewing empire were laid. It is still controlled by the Busch family.

Most of the United States's big breweries have Germanic origins and four of them take their place amongst the top ten of the world's largest brewing companies: Anheuser-Busch, Miller, Stroh and Coors.

It comes as no surprise to find that the USA is the world's major beer producer, brewing more than one hundred and forty five million barrels of beer each year. It is, however, well down the list in personal consumption of beer with its one hundred and sixty pints per head falling well behind the Czechs at almost double that figure. The Canadians drink even less at one hundred and forty five pints each year.

LAGER, LAGER, EVERYWHERE
Most of the leading brands of the major brewers are pale, bottom fermenting lagers, consequently this style dominates North American beer drinking. However, the explosion of micro-breweries in the last two decades has led to the revival of many old styles and the import of others mainly from Europe. But lager continues to hold sway.

Adolphus Busch returned to Europe in 1876 and brought back a lager style beer from the town of Budweis in Bohemia. He called it Budweiser and today it is one of the world's best selling beers. There have been legal wrangles over the years because of its name and a similarly titled beer from the Czech home town. The American version is a sweetly hopped, thinnish drink with a strength of 4.5% abv. It is universally exported.

Another major brewer Coors, based in Golden, Colorado, has a flagship lager, simply called Coors, which is clean tasting and widely exported. Miller beers along with the other major brewers' lagers also reach beyond America's shores.

But happily the small breweries have also made their mark both at home and in the export field. The Samuel Adams brewery in Boston has Boston Lager as its mainstream beer. It is aromatic and spicey and very easily drinkable. Surprisingly it is made in Portland and Pittsburgh and not in Boston but the home brewery does produce a range of speciality beers.

In Philadelphia the Dock Street Brewery

Chilli beer from the USA

Celis White Beer, Austin, Texas

Above right: Samuel Adams Boston Lager

produces a whole range of lagers including Oscura a dark, Mexican type. It also brews a Bohemian Pils in the Czech manner and a light, hoppy German Pils. Carol Stroudt who brews in Adamstown, Pennsylvania, also has a large portfolio of beers which includes a gently hopped Pilsner and an aromatic Export Gold.

Whilst Canada tends to mirror the United States in its brewing culture there are some distinct differences. Canadian lagers are usually slightly higher in strength than their counterparts in the USA.

Neither of the two major brewers – Labatt and Molson – produce a lager of great distinction. But there are some good examples from amongst the smaller companies. Big Rock's XO Lager from Calgary, Alberta, is one of them. It is a splendidly crafted beer with dry spicey flavours. And at Creemore, 100 miles west of Toronto, the hoppy Creemore Springs Premium Lager is well thought of.

ALE, GLORIOUS ALE

Ale is probably the fastest growing style of beer in the United States and whilst some of the major brewers are now experimenting, it is the small breweries that win the awards.

One of the best known is from the Anchor Brewing Company

Below right: Beers from the Anchor Steam Brewery, San Francisco

Beers devised by Pete Celis

of San Francisco, better known for its Steam Beer. But Anchor Liberty Ale with a strength of 6.0% has a robust nature and a character that picks it out of the ruck. Anchor Brewing dates from the nineteenth century but underwent a revival in the 1960s.

Pete Slosberg created his Pete's Wicked Ale after a visit to Britain and an experience of real ale. It is brewed in St Paul, Minnesota, is dark and rich and is exported to Britain. It won the gold medal for brown ale at the Great American Beer Festival in 1992. He brews to Reinheitsgebot standards.

Eye of Hawl (6.5%) from the Mendicino Brewing Company at the appropriately named Hopland in California is another prize winner. This rich malty ale with a clean dry finish took the bronze medal for strong ales at the 1992 Great American Beer Festival.

The Steelhead Brewery at Eugene, Oregon, make two ales of character: the dry hoppy Emerald Special Bitter and the assertive Bombay Bomber. At Chico in Northern California the Sierra Nevada brewery produces two classic ales: the sweetish Sierra Nevada Draught Ale and the intensely hoppy, magnificent Pale Ale. Other brewers have much praise for the Pale Ale and it is difficult to understand why such a beer is not exported.

At Bert Grant's brewery at Yakima in Washington state's hop

country, a whole series of ales is produced. Celtic Ale is dark and hoppy but not of the Irish tradition; Grant's Ale claims to share the maker's Scottish ancestry although lacking the sweetness; and IPA (India Pale Ale) is an entirely appropriate name to its intense hoppy nature. All three are excellent beers.

The English pale ale style is being copied extensively in the USA with Cascade hops from Oregon and Washington State being used to provide flavour and bouquet.

In the eastern states the Catamount Brewery at White River Junction in Vermont produces a rich Amber Ale with an aggressive hop character and plenty of bite. Another Amber Ale comes from the Manhattan Brewing Company's brew pub in New York. It is a well rounded, fruity beer and partners the dry, slightly stronger IPA.

STOUTS AND OTHER SPECIALTIES

Stouts and Porters have a long tradition in the United States although it was becoming a forgotten style. Several micros have revived it and Miller, the nation's second largest brewer, recently introduced its Velvet Stout: a rather thin beer but smooth and pleasant to drink.

The Alaskan Brewing Company is located in Juneau, capital of America's Arctic state. Each Christmas it brews a Smoked Porter with the help of a salmon smoke house neighbour. It is rich with an intense smokiness and could lay claim to be a style of its own.

McAuslans Brewing in Montreal produce St Ambrose Oatmeal Stout (5.5%) with all-Canadian ingredients except the yeast which is shipped from England. Oatmeal is used in the mash and the beer is smooth, dry and very chewy.

The strongest beer in North America is Sierra Nevada's Big Foot Barley Wine at 12.5% abv. This very hoppy beer continues to condition in the bottle after a four week stay in the brewery and is probably at its best after a year or so.

Attempts to copy the Lambic and Gueuze beers of Belgium have not been successful in the United States although some excellent fruit beers have been created by the use of other styles of brewing.

The Samuel Adams brewery in Boston make use of local fruit to produce the confusingly named Cranberry Lambic. Lambic it isn't, for these beers require the use of a spontaneously fermented beer at their base and this one uses a wheat beer. But tart and fruity it certainly is. Martin Brewing in the Bay area of San Francisco brew a Raspberry Wheat Beer and Spinnakers in Victoria, British Columbia a Dunkel Krieken Weizen which is flavoured with cherries.

Wheat beers in the Munich, Berlin and Belgian styles are found all over the United States. In Washington State at Poulsbo near Seattle, Thomas Kemper's Hefe-Weizen is brewed and at Kalama the Hefeweizen of the Pyramid brewery.

In the opposite corner of the United States in Austin, Texas, the wonderful Celis White is brewed. It is a refreshing, aromatic drink of great character. The brewery was established by Pieter

Celis who revived wheat beer brewing in the 1960s at Hoegaarden in Belgium before emigrating to the USA. He has since returned to Belgium and it is rumoured that he is about to set up a third brewery.

If there is a quintessential style of beer for the United States it is steam beer and particularly the unique Anchor Steam Beer brewed in San Francisco. This combines the styles of ale and lager and is bottom-fermented in shallow vessels from an all-malt brew. It is only 5.0% abv in strength but has a complex make-up with wonderful aromas and flavours.

LATIN AMERICA AND THE CARIBBEAN

Most of the beer culture of Latin and South America is Germanic. Bohemian and Bavarian brewers were shipped across the Atlantic in the nineteenth century along with Austrian Emperors, Irish revolutionaries and British railway engineers. As a consequence most beers today are pilsner in style with occasional forays into the dark lagers of Bavaria. Little else exists except in the Caribbean where a number of porters and stouts are brewed.

Both Brazil and Mexico take their place in the world's top ten beer producers. Beer is a popular drink in these and many other countries of the region. Mexico has the widest selection of beers although most of these are bland tasting lagers.

Mexico's best known beer is Corona followed closely by Sol. Both are bland, fizzy medium gravity beers which are often

Red Stripe from Jamaica

Above: Dos Equis from Mexico

Right: Xingu Black Beer is brewed at Cacador, Brazil and is exported to Europe and The USA

Below: Jamaica's Dragon Stout is supposed to help increase male virility

Opposite: Rio carnival passing the Brahma brewery

drunk with a slice of lemon or lime to add flavour. Other breweries produce similar beers and they have become popular in the US border states.

If these light characterless beers can be identified as a Mexican style then fortunately there are alongside them a few genuine lagers and pilsners to drink. Bohemia is a full-flavoured pilsner and Dos Equis is in the reddish Vienna style. Commemorative and Noche Buena are dark Christmas beers with strengths around 5.5%.

The Caribbean islands are something of a different picture. Universally known is Jamaica's Red Stripe Lager which is now brewed in Britain to satisfy the thirst of many West Indian immigrants and their descendants. It is a smooth, lightly hopped beer with a strength of 4.8% abv produced by Desnoes and Geddes a long established local company. Also in their portfolio are the stronger Crucial Lager and the sweet and rich Dragon Stout.

Right: Labels from Guatemala and Costa Rica

Below: Atlas beer from Panama

Left: Labels from Uruguay

At Spanish Town in Jamaica is the Central Village Brewery where Guinness Stout is brewed under contract. There are similar breweries on the islands of Trinidad, Granada and St Vincent. The stouts are usually considerably stronger than those produced in London and Dublin.

Most of the lagers brewed in the Caribbean islands are not attenuated for long, say two weeks, which accounts for their sweeter than the average taste. However Carib lager from Trinidad bucks the trend by being relatively dry and Bank's lager of Barbados is much fuller in flavour than other similar beers. Banks also have a brewery in Guyana on the South American mainland.

In some of the French islands the *bières de garde* style of north-east France are popular although they are mostly imports. The Lorraine Brewery on Martinique brews a range of 'homeland' beers as well as the more ethnic lagers. On Haiti a favourite drink is Prestige Stout, a very dry beer, although not very strong.

Throughout South America a series of local breweries produce similar tasting lagers of little consequence and of not much interest to drinkers from other lands. Polar lager from Venezuela is exported as is Aguila. Others include Cordoba in Argentina, Cristal from Chile, Colombia's Bavaria and Brahma from Brazil.

Brazil also produces an unusual dark beer called Xingu which lays some pretentious claims on links with the Amazonian Indians. It is a jet black beer quite unlike stout with lots of fruity flavour. It is exported into the United States from where it is financed and also to Europe. Xingu is brewed at Cacador in the south-eastern province of Santa Catarina which is, incidentally, almost two thousand miles from the Amazon River.

AUSTRALIA AND NEW ZEALAND

N ew Zealanders are the southern hemisphere's champion beer drinkers, downing one hundred and eighty five pints each year on average. They are followed closely by the Australians and both nations take a comfortable place in the top ten of the world's drinkers.

The first brewery in Australia was built in 1794. A century later there were some twenty-five breweries and by then all of them had dropped the British ale and stout styles in favour of bottom-fermented lager. This remains the favoured style to this day usually drunk very cold and from cans. The theory, not admitted by Australians, is that thirsts have to be quenched and the taste of the beer is unimportant. But some small changes are being noted.

Two main groups dominate the Australian market and both export vast quantities of their beers. Two main groups dominate the New Zealand market and both export vast quantities of their beers. One brewer – Lion Nathan, a New Zealand company – takes its place in both these pairings.

Lion Nathan in its own land is better known as New Zealand Breweries and the hoppy, spritzy Steinlager which sells across the world is its brand leader. It won second prize in its class at the 1995 Brewing Industry International Awards at Burton upon Trent in the UK. There is also a lesser gravity local lager called Rheineck. The group has three breweries at Auckland, Hastings and Christchurch. Lion also owns three of Australia's major breweries: Castelmains XXXX is available in Britain where it is brewed and promoted by Carlsberg-Tetley the brewing arm of Allied Domecq. It is a lager but sells in Australia as Bitter Ale. There is also a Carbine Stout which is dry and malty.

Opposite: James Boag's Premium Lager, Launceston, Tasmania

Right: Foster's, designed to be drunk cool

FOSTER'S EXPORT STOUT

F

FOSTER'S

· BREWED & BOTTLED BY ·
CARLTON & UNITED
BREWERIES
LIMITED.
A6FS
· MELBOURNE | AUSTRALIA ·

BREWED FROM PUREST MALT & HOPS

SANDS & McDOUGALL PTY LTD

Above Left: Beers from Coopers, Adelaide, South Australia

There are three breweries of which the main one is in Brisbane.

Both Swan in Perth, Western Australia, and Toohey's in Sydney produce a range of fairly uninspired lagers although the latter does brew a dark beer, Old Black, which has a toffee flavour and a sharp bite.

Toohey's is known in Sydney as the Catholic or Irish brewery whereas Tooth's, the city's other major brewer, is the Protestant or English brewery. Tooth's has a range of lagers plus a Sheaf Stout and a top fermenting brown ale. It is part of the Foster group, the country's other major brewer.

Foster's largest brewery is in Melbourne and, for the moment, it also owns the Courage Brewing empire in Great Britain and Foster's Lager is brewed there. Again there is a range of lager style beers, often called 'bitters' and a stout which is bottom-fermented.

Left: Steinlager, a Pilsner-type beer from New Zealand which is widely exported

Opposite: A classic poster from Boag's of Tasmania

Coopers Sparkling Ale is much enjoyed by
fashion conscious Australians

THE RARE TOP FERMENTERS

Top fermentation is rare in Australia except in the small clutch
of mini and pub breweries. One honourable exception is the old
established independent company, Cooper's of Adelaide in South
Australia. It brews a range of fine, fruity beers, some of which
are exported.

Cooper's Original is the best known but the slightly stronger
Cooper's Sparkling Ale has more body and assertiveness. In a
more European style but stronger than expected are the dark Ale
and Best Extra Stout. The founder of the firm, Thomas Cooper,
was a Yorkshireman who emigrated to Australia in the
nineteenth century and his descendants still run the company.

There are two breweries on the island of Tasmania where much
of Australia's barley and hops are grown. Cascade which started
brewing in 1824 is the oldest in the nation. It also owns the
other Tasmanian brewery: Boag's. All the beers are bottom-
fermented and most of them are lagers.

New Zealand's other major group is Dominion Breweries with
three plants at Waitemata near Auckland, and Timaru and
Greymouth on the south island. At the 1994 Brewing Industry
International Awards at Burton upon Trent in England
Dominion picked up three first prizes, two seconds and two
third prizes in the lager classes and two first prizes and a
second in the ale classes.

There is a claim that Captain James Cook, who discovered
the country in 1773, was New Zealand's first brewer. He is
said to have satisfied the thirsts of his crew, and himself, by
concocting a brew from fermented sugars and flavouring it with
herbs and tea!

ASIA
AND AFRICA

Western style beers which were introduced to Japan and taken up with great enthusiasm in the middle of the nineteenth century have remained the favourites. Now the country ranks fourth in the world's major beer producers. The Japanese brewing industry is probably the most technically advanced in the world.

Of the forty three million barrels brewed each year there is little choice of style and ninety-eight per cent of it comes from just four companies: Kirin, Asahi, Sapporo and Suntory which between them operates twenty nine breweries. Until recently there was a minimum limit to the amount brewed for a company to obtain a brewing licence. Now this has changed and an explosion of mini- breweries and brew-pubs can be expected as Japan belatedly joins the beer renaissance.

But while European pilsner and lager styles dominate the market each of the four large groups have interesting beers in their portfolios. Kirin for example produces a Black Beer with smokey undertones almost in the Bamberg fashion and also a 10.0%

Solan brewery, Simla Road, India. Possibly the highest brewery in the world

Above right: Kingfisher lager, India

Right: Beers from the Lion brewery, Sri Lanka

beer called Ad Lib, the label of which invites the drinker to 'dilute to taste.'

Sapporo also brews a toffee flavoured and nutty Black Beer as well as several specialities that follow German styles. Asahi brews a Stout which is powerful and follows the English tradition. And Suntory produces a spicey Weizen, a German type wheat beer. International beers such as Guinness, Budweiser and Carlsberg are brewed in Japan under licence.

China is now the third largest beer producer in the world. Production has multiplied six times in the last ten years and many other large brewing nations, such as Japan, Britain and Brazil have been overtaken. Yet little is known of the industry with small local breweries serving their own communities with beers that satisfy local tastes.

The Chinese brewery best known in the west is Tsingtao at the Yellow Sea resort of Qingdao in the Shandong province. It was set up with American capital and its beers are widely exported to the west. The popular Tsingtao Beer is a hoppy pilsner which is a good accompaniment to Chinese food.

There are breweries in many Asian countries except in the most strict of Muslim nations although like China few of their beers reach outside their bounds. The exceptions are beers such as the very sharp tasting Singha Lager from Thailand which is appearing in Britain in the burgeoning Thai restaurant trade; Tiger Beer from Singapore and Malaysia, strong and hoppy and beloved of British soldiers and sailors who served in these lands.

THE BRITISH INFLUENCE

The Indian sub continent deserves greater mention. The industry displays traces of its British origins and in Sri

Above: Beers from Asia

Lanka there are still bars using hand pumps to dispense top fermented beers.

India has a thriving brewing industry with some thirty breweries serving the large nation and also exporting mainly to countries where its nationals have emigrated to – Britain in particular. Some Indian beers are now being brewed under contract in Britain. These include the popular Kingfisher lager and the recently introduced Lal Tofal which includes some rice in its mash.

The highest brewery in the world is at Solan in the Himalayan foothills close to Simla where the British Raj would resort to in summer from Calcutta. It was built to satisfy British thirsts and shares its site with a distillery. It stands around eight thousand feet above sea level and brews a sweetish malty lager. It is the type of beer that most Indian brewers produce; some make dark beers as well and others make stouts but most bars including the open air beer shops concentrate on pale lagers.

The British influence is also seen at Rawalpindi in Pakistan where the Murree brewery produces a London Lager with Nelson's column on its label as well as a stronger Export Lager and a stout.

Left: Kirin, Japan's largest brewery

Above right: Tiger Lager Beer, Singapore

Below: Sable

Right: Singha Lager from Thailand

Sri Lanka beers have become better known as some of the Lion brand have been exported to western nations. Its breweries are well established with two main ones – Ceylon Breweries (Lion) and McCallum – taking most of the trade.

Lion Stout is top-fermented and sold in bottles and locally in wooden casks. In some beer cafes it is served by hand pump. It is very dark with wonderful burnt malt and chocolate flavours. Lion Lager is also dispensed by hand pump and both beers are exported. McCallum have a similar range: Sando Stout and Three Coins Pilsner.

One Sri Lankan beer that is not exported is the locally produced 'Toddy' which is made from the sap of the coconut palm and takes just a few hours to ferment. It is said to be tart and soapy yet with a sweet finish and looking and smelling like sour milk!

THE BIRTHPLACE OF BREWING

There are claims that in Egypt six thousand years ago the first beers were brewed. What is certain is that brewing in Africa did not develop from those early beginnings. Beers brewed across this vast continent in around two hundred and fifty breweries are all influenced by the mass market beers of Europe dating from the years of colonialism.

In Egypt they still brew a beer called Stella which was much loved by British troops stationed there during and after the Second World War. But cold light beers have always been the taste of Europeans in hot climates and much of Africa's brewing industry produces this style. Native Africans tend to prefer cold dark beers such as high gravity stouts brewed by Guinness and that company has a substantial presence in Africa.

Nigeria is Africa's major brewing nation with four Guinness breweries: two in Benin and others at Ikeja and Ogba. There are other major groups – Golden Guinea in Imo State is the largest locally owned brewery, and Nigerian Breweries in which Heineken has a stake has bases in Aba, Kaduna and Lagos.

There are also Guinness breweries in Ghana and Cameroun and others licensed to brew in Liberia and Sierra Leone.

Above left: South African Breweries
Above right: Tusker

Kenya has a well established brewery formed by a group of expatriate British farmers in 1922. Kenya Breweries has developed into one of the best known in Africa mainly for its Tusker lagers which are exported. There are breweries in Mombasa, Kisamu and Nairobi. Its parent company is East Africa Breweries which also owns a brewery in Uganda.

South Africa is the continent's second largest producer of beers although most of the beers are in the lager style and brewed by one company. South African Breweries was established in 1895 and it sells its beers under the Lion and Castle labels. Guinness have a small operation here but, for the moment, are not brewing although this is likely in the near future. And there are now two micro brewers one at Knysna in Cape Province, the other in Johannesburg. Others are expected to follow.

Africa has some unique beers, usually brewed in homes or in the beer halls of the South African townships. These 'kaffir' beers are porridge-like, thick and cloying with a sour flavour. In Burkino Faso the beer is called Dolo and there are similar types elsewhere across the continent. Millet and cassava are used in the mash and their sole objective appears to be to achieve insobriety!

Above: Rong Cheng beers from the Fujian brewery, China

135

TOP TEN BEERS

Selecting these ten beers was an almost impossible task. My first list had twenty-seven beers on it. I cut these down to sixteen. And then, after much soul searching, to thirteen. It took me a long time from there. In the end I had to leave out one of my very favourite beers and I feel that I can never forgive myself. So here is what remains, in ascending order of strength with their styles and the places in which they are brewed:

TETLEY MILD, 3.2%, Draught Mild Ale, Leeds, England

TAYLOR LANDLORD, 4.3%, Draught Premium Bitter Ale, Keighley, West Yorks, England

MARSTON PEDIGREE, 4.5%, Draught Pale Ale, Burton upon Trent, Staffordshire, England

SAMUEL ADAMS BOSTON LAGER, 4.8%, Bottled Lager, Boston, Mass, USA

BUDWEISER BUDVAR, 5.0%, Draught and bottled Budvar Lager, Ceske Budejovice, Czech Republic

ANCHOR STEAM BEER, 5.0%, Bottled Steam Beer, San Francisco, Cal., USA

SCHNEIDER WEISSE, 5.3%, Bottled Wheat Beer, Kelheim, Bavaria, Germany

ORVAL, 6.2%, Bottled Trappist Ale, Villers-devant-Orval, Belgium

GUINNESS FOREIGN EXTRA STOUT, 7.5%, Bottled Dry Stout, Dublin, Ireland

ELDRIDGE POPE THOMAS HARDY ALE, 12.0%, Bottle Conditioned Strong Ale, Dorchester, Dorset, England

A GLOSSARY OF BEERS AND BREWING

Alcoholic strength: This can be measured in various ways but the acceptable standard is now 'alcohol by volume' (abv) which is also the method used to measure the alcohol in wine and spirits.

Ale: Originally it meant an unhopped beverage and this distinguished it from beer. However the terms are now synonymous although beer tends to be used as the generic term and ale is not taken to include such beers as lager and stout.

Barley: The essential first stage in making beer is to grow good barley, and then convert it into malt.

Barrel: see Cask.

Beer: The generic term for alcoholic drinks made from malted barley and sometimes other fermentable materials, that are flavoured and preserved with hops.

Bottle-conditioned ale: A beer that goes through a secondary fermentation in the bottle. It produces a sediment and requires care in storing and pouring.

Bright beer: A term often used for beers that have been chilled and filtered or pasteurised leaving them without life. Similar to keg or brewery-conditioned beer. The antithesis of 'real ale'.

Burtonise: The method of adding salts (usually calcium sulphate) to brewing water to make it similar to the natural well water of Burton upon Trent for the brewing of bitter beers and pale ales.

CAMRA: The Campaign for Real Ale; 'Europe's most successful consumer organisation', was formed in 1971 to combat the slide away from traditional beers to national keg brands. It now has 50,000 members, mainly in Britain, and campaigns on other issues including takeovers, pub closures and beer prices.

Caramel: Roasted sugar which may be added to give colour and some sweetness to beers.

Carbon dioxide (CO₂): A gas produced naturally by the action of yeast on beer wort. It is essential to keep beer in good condition but added CO_2 can give beer a fizzy quality and unpleasant flavours.

Cask: The general name given to a container for draught beer. It can either be wood or metal. Another generalised term is barrel but strictly this is a cask containing 36 gallons and the standard by which production is measured.

Cask conditioned: Beer that undergoes a secondary fermentation in the cask and is improved as a result. Another term for Real Ale (qv).

Chilled and filtered: A process for producing bright beer (qv) by which the beer is chilled so that the proteins are separated out and then filtered to leave a clear beer.

Conditioning: Allowing beer to reach its optimum quality in the cellar. Achieving the correct stage in cask conditioned (qv) beers is a skilled job.

Cooper: The trade of making and repairing wooden casks. Few such craftsmen are found these days in the brewing industry.

Copper: The vessel in which the wort (qv) and the hops are boiled prior to fermentation. Sometimes called the kettle.

Decoction: The method of mashing used in lager brewing. (See also Mashing).

Draught or Draft (US): Strictly, beer that is 'drawn' from a cask but the term is used generally to mean any bulk beer and is now increasingly and confusingly being used for bottled and canned beers.

Dry hopping: Adding a handful of hops to a cask when it is filled with beer. This gives a distinct aroma to the beer.

Fermentation: The action of yeast on beer wort which produces alcohol and carbon dioxide.

Finings: A substance made from the swim bladder of a sturgeon which is added to beer during conditioning to allow it to drop clear.

Gyle: A batch of beer from a single brewing. It is usually given a 'gyle number' which is then marked on the cask.

Hand pump: Sometimes called 'hand pull'. A popular name for a beer engine which draws beer from the cellar to the bar.

Hops: The flowers of a climbing plant which adds bitterness to beers and also acts as a preservative. English hops are traditionally grown in the south-east and south midlands and those from the USA in Washington and Oregon. New Zealand, Tazmania,the Czech Republic and Germany are other hop producing nations.

Liquor: What the brewer calls the water used to make beer.

Malt: The main essential of beer - barley (and occasionally other cereals) which has gone through the process of partial germination and kilning.

Maltings: A place where barley is converted into malt.

Original gravity: The system used until recently in Britain to determine the amount of duty payable on beer. It was a rough guide to strength.

Priming: The addition of sugar to certain brews to start a secondary fermentation.

Real Ale: A term coined by CAMRA meaning beer brewed from traditional ingredients, matured by a secondary fermentation in the cask and served without the use of extraneous carbon dioxide. Sometimes called 'traditional' or cask'. (see also Cask-conditioned.)

Reinheitsgebot: The German beer purity law dating from 1516. It allows only malted barley or wheat, hops and yeast to be used in brewing. Not even sugar is allowed.

Tower brewery: The traditional style of brewery common to the nineteenth century many of which are still in use. Water is raised to the top floor and the various brewing processes flow downwards by gravity.

Wort: The liquid produced by mashing together liquor (water) and malt - this is known as the sweet wort - after boiling with hops it becomes the hopped wort.

Yeast: A single-celled fungus which, when pitched on to wort, produces alcohol and carbon dioxide. It is the 'magic' property in beer making. Breweries often retain their yeast strains for many years.

Zymurgy: The art and science of brewing

INDEX

PICTURE CREDITS